VATICAN

History and Art

MONUMENTI MUSEI E GALLERIE PONTIFICIE

Vatican City. To the left (south) of the basilica is the large cement building of the Hall of Papal Audiences. To the right (north) of the basilica are the Sistine Chapel, the medieval palace of the popes with Bramante's Loggias and, lower down, the present Apostolic Palace. Further north are the Vatican Museums. Higher up, in the gardens, are the Palazzina of Leo XIII and the Fontana dell'Aquilone.

▷

Vatican City. To the left (north) of the basilica is the Sistine Chapel and, opposite it, the building of Pius V, next to the medieval palace of the popes and the Borgia Tower. To the left of the palace and the tower stands the Belvedere Courtyard. In the gardens are the Leonine Tower and, below it, the Palazzina of Leo XIII, today the Vatican Radio; below the apse of the basilica is the Palace of the Government.

*On the cover: St. Peter's Square.
Inside front- and back-cover. Ignazio Danti: Map of Rome, detail of the Vatican, Gallery of Maps. The Sacristy of St. Peter's at the end of the XVIII century, fresco in the hemicycle of the Etruscan Museum.
Frontispiece: The Swiss Guards.
Back-cover: Bronze statue of St. Peter enthroned, attributed to Arnolfo di Cambio. St. Peter's.*

* * * * * *

© COPYRIGHT 1974 by SCALA Istituto Fotografico Editoriale, Firenze
Text: Fabrizio Mancinelli
Translation: Lisa Clark
Editorial Director: Francesco Papafava
Editors: Barbara Gökgöl, Daniele Casalino
Layout: Fried Rosenstock
Photopgraphs: SCALA (Angelo Corsini, Mario Falsini and Mauro Sarri), except on p. 2 (Publiaerfoto), p. 3 (F. Quilici), pp. 5, 37 (Vatican Museus), p. 7 (Alinari), pp. 8, 22, 53 (Vatican Library), pp. 22, 64 (P. De Antonis), p. 23 (Lichtbildwerkstätte « Alpenland », © Albertina, Graphische Sammlung, Wien), p. 44 (Kupferstichkabinett Berlin)
Produced by SCALA with the authorization and the cooperation of the Direzione Generale dei Musei Vaticani, and: Biblioteca Apostolica Vaticana; Pontificia Commissione per le Comunicazioni Sociali; Pontificia Commissione per lo Stato della Città del Vaticano; Reverenda Fabbrica di San Pietro
Printed in Italy by Sogema Marzari
Schio 1984

INDEX

The Vatican City stands near the right bank of the Tiber on high ground which once formed the ancient "ager Vaticanus. The Emperor Caligula (37-41 A.D.) built a Circus there, to the left of where the basilica of St. Peter's now stands, and placed in it the Egyptian obelisk now in the centre of the square. Nero (54-68 A.D.) enlarged the Circus and it was there and in the neighbouring gardens that he had the first Christian martyrs tortured, in 64 A.D. Among those martyred was St. Peter. To the north of the Circus and separated from it by a road, there was a slope, and on the top of the slope a necropolis, which was even at that time ancient. Here the prince of the apostles was burried. Over his tomb the Emperor Constantine (306-337) erected after 324, probably in 330, a majestic basilica, for which the pre-

sent basilica was built, between the fifteenth and seventeenth centuries, as a replacement. During the Middle Ages a few buildings were constructed next to the basilica, but the popes only resided in them temporarily and usually because of an unstable political situation, which had forced them to withdraw from their normal residence, the Lateran. In the ninth century, Leo IV built a circle of walls around the area, until that time in open country-side, trasforming the Vatican into a secure fortified citadel. In the thirteenth century, Nicholas III, who lived permanently in the Vatican, built the first real pontifical palace. This palace-cum-fortress, built on a rectangular plan (cf. p. 22), probably had defensive towers at each corner. It was built around a courtyard, known today as the Courtyard of the Pappagallo, and

incorporated to the south a fortified construction built by Innocent III north of the basilica. In 1377, after the return of Gregory XI from his exile in Avignon, the Vatican became the permanent residence of the popes and, in the following century with Nicholas V (cf. p. 28), a very grand programme of renovation was begun. The Apostolic Palace was modified and Nicholas V completed the north wing; to him we also owe the project for the enlarge-ment of St. Peter's. Sixtus IV (cf. p. 30) is responsible for the Sistine Chapel (cf. p. 31) and the definitive arrange-ment of the Vatican Library, already begun by Nicholas V. During the papacy of Innocent VIII (cf. p. 16) a summer residence, the Palazzetto del Belvedere (cf. p. 44), was built on the hill north of the palace. During the last decade of the fifteenth century,

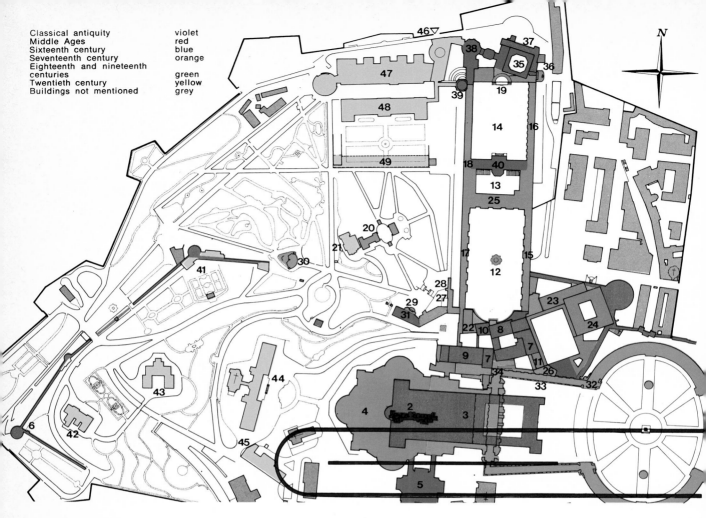

Alexander VI Borgia (cf. p. 30) had the Borgia Tower built and also had the apartment on the first floor (cf. p. 29) of the north wing of the palace decorated by Pinturicchio.

With Julius II (cf. p. 34), the original complex of the Apostolic Palace was given, through the work of Bramante, a renaissance appearance (cf. p. 22, 23). The architect planned to connect the Apostolic Palace to the Palazzetto del Belvedere with a grandiose courtyard, the Belvedere Courtyard (cf. p. 2). He also altered the plan of the palace in the side facing Rome: he hid the medieval facade built by Nicholas III with three rows of loggias. Also drawn up by Bramante was the first real project for the reconstruction of St. Peter's. Among the works of decoration commissioned by Julius II are the ceiling of the Sistine Chapel (cf. p. 32), painted by Michelangelo, and the frescoes in the pope's own apartments, on the second floor of the north wing of the palace, by Raphael. Leo X, his successor, also entrusted to Raphael the decoration of Bramante's Loggias (cf. p. 36).

With Paul III, Antonio da Sangallo was given the task of remodernizing the south wing of the old palace, to be used for public ceremonies (cf. p. 27). Paul III also commissioned the Last Judgment (cf. p. 33) in the Sistine Chapel from Michelangelo, ordering that this fresco should have precedence over the reconstruction of St. Peter's (cf. p. 10, 11). During the second half of the sixteenth century, under Pius IV, the west wing and the north facade of the Belvedere Courtyard, with the famous Nicchione, were completed (cf. p. 47). The architect of these plans was Pirro Ligorio, from whom the pope also commissioned the Casina (cf. p. 54, 55), an important example of mannerist architecture, which today houses the Papal Academy of Science. Gregory XIII had the palace on the north side of the Courtyard of St. Damasus (cf. p. 23) built; the facade of this building is a continuation of Bramante's Loggias. This pope also commissioned from Ottaviano Mascherino tre construction of the Gallery of Maps (cf. p. 38) and the Tower of Winds above it (cf. p. 40), the first

Above left: the Tribunal Palace, the railway station and the Government Palace.

Above right: the Vatican Gardens, and the Palazzina of Leo XIII with Vatican Radio.

Below left: the Hall of Papal Audiences and the Sacristy.

Below center: St. John's Tower.

Below right: the Tower of Nicholas V and Vatican Radio.

Vatican observatory. Sixtus V entrusted to Domenico Fontana the building of the new Apostolic Palace (cf. p. 22), which to this day is the residence of the popes, closing in on the east side the Courtyard of St. Damasus (cf. p. 23). Also to Domenico Fontana we owe the new building of the Vatican Library where the Salone Sistino (cf. p. 42) now is and which cuts across the Belvedere Courtyard (cf. p. 2, 56).

In the seventeenth century, during the papacy of Paul V, the construction of St. Peter's (cf. p. 6) was completed. This pope also commissioned the building under which the Stradone ai Giardini, which leads to the museums (cf. p. 56), passes; he endowed the palace with a monumental entrance, of which the Bronze Door (cf. p. 25) still stands, and embellished the gardens with many fountains (cf. p. 51, 52, 53). Alexander VII entrusted to Gian Lorenzo Bernini the building of the colonnade (cf. p. 7) of St. Peter's Square and the Scala Regia (cf. p. 26). With Benedict XIV (cf. p. 57) the history of the museums begins: in 1756 he founded the Sacred Museum of the Vatican Library. In 1767, Clement XIII (cf. p. 20) founded the Profane Museum of the Vatican Library. Under the auspices of Clement XIV and Pius VI, the architects Michelangelo Simonetti and Giuseppe Camporese built the Pio-Clementine Museum (cf. p. 45), transforming completely the Palazzetto del Belvedere. In the following century, Pius VII continued the work of his predecessors, by commissioning Pasquale Belli to build the Braccio

Nuovo, on a project by Raffaello Stern. During this century, with Pius XI, a new construction programme was begun, in part due to the new status of the Vatican after the 1929 treaty, which risolved the complex controversy between the Holy See and Italy which had arisen after the conquest of Rome (1870). In 1931 Guglielmo Marconi set up the Vatican Radio, and in 1929 Luca Beltrami built the Pinacoteca. Also new buildings for the administration of the new state were built, including the Palace of the Government, by Giuseppe Momo. To John XXIII (cf. p. 21) and Paul VI we owe the building which houses the collections formerly in the Lateran (cf. p. 60, 61) and the Hall of Papal Audiences (cf. p. 63).

The square and basilica of St. Peter's. To the right of the basilica are the Sistine Chapel and the Apostolic Palace.
▷
St. Peter's Square, Via della Conciliazione, Castel Sant'Angelo and the Tiber seen from the dome of the basilica.
▷
St. Peter's Square and the Borgo before the demolition of the Spina (1937).

The facade of St. Peter's was built by Carlo Maderno between 1608 and 1612, during the papacy of Paul V, but remained without the planned bell-towers; these were designed to draw attention to the cupola and thus to lighten somewhat the effect of the whole. Gian Lorenzo Bernini put forward his solution of the problem in 1637: twin bell-towers with columns at each corner and crowned by spires, each one in all 100 metres high. During the construction of the left tower, subsidence occurred in the portico and the project was therefore abandoned. With Innocent X, the successor of Urban VIII (cf. p. 20), Bernini fell into disgrace and the bell-tower was removed. But, after the death of Innocent X in 1655, Alexander VII recalled the artist and entrusted him with the task of transforming the square facing the basilica into a huge atrium, with the obelisk from Caligula's Circus in the middle. Some of the work had in fact already been done by Domenico Fontana as early as 1586. On 28 August 1656 the pope placed the first stone; 140 statues of

saints crown the work which was completed in a decade. The huge ellyptical semicircular square was built originally to face the church rather than the city. At the end of the two arms of colonnades, a central sector was designed to leave open two side entrances. The two straight wings that join the colonnades to the church have the function of making the church seem closer to the square than it is. Also, Maderno's portal, which was universally considered too low, was made to seem larger and higher by the colonnade.

The dynamic effect of church and square was considerably changed by the construction of Via della Conciliazione. The demolition in 1937 of the Spina quarter, so called because of its peculiar shape, has in fact inverted the effect envisaged by Bernini. Several famous buildings were involved in the demolition, notably the Palazzo dell'Aquila (perhaps by Raphael) and the Palazzo dei Penitenzieri.

8

St. Peter's. Niche for the consecration of the episcopal robes.

◁
Jacopo Grimaldi: Constantine's basilica (drawing of the second half of the sixteenth century; the side porticoes had already been lost).

◁
Vatican Grottoes (St. Peter's). The Chapel of St. Peter. Beyond the grate at the far side is the lower part of the marble altar of Constantine.

The basilica of St. Peter's stands on the slopes of the hill of the Vatican, on the site of the basilica built by Constantine and of the apostle's tomb. He was buried "in humili sepultura", in a ditch hollowed in the bare earth and covered by a few tiles, not far from the place of his martyrdom, in a pagan cemetery. In the second century a monument was built on the place: two niches were placed over one another, against a wall. Constantine's architects built the basilica with five naves, aligning it with the monument, over the pagan necropolis, which was partially razed and filled with débris to create a level surface. In front of the facade, which was decorated with mosaics, there was a courtyard surrounded by colonnades, in the centre of which Pope Symmachus in the sixth century built a basin for ablutions, and the stone pine cone, now in the Courtyard of the Pigna. The apostle's monument was left visible at the centre of the transept and the papal altar was built over it; its lower niche corresponds today to the niche for the consecration of the episcopal robes. The mosaic of Christ, which has been much restored, was made after Leo III. The figures of St. Peter and St. Paul are of the time of Urban VIII. The casket for the robes is of the time of Benedict XIV. Above the niche is a grille with an inscription of Innocent III, behind which, on a table of oak, were fitted the statuettes in enamel of Limoges representing Christ and the twelve apostles, today partly in the Sacred Museum in the Vatican Library.

The place nearest to the tomb of St. Peter is the chapel of the same name, also known as the Clementine Chapel, because it was restored under Clement VIII, in the Vatican Grottoes at more or less the same level as Constantine's basilica. The chapel dates from the time of Gregory I, who had the floor of the apse raised, making the first basilica with a raised presbytery.

9

St. Peter's. The dome, the transept and the apse.

During the Middle Ages Constantine's basilica underwent numerous changes and additions. But in the fifteenth century it was no longer big enough and, most important of all, its structure had become unsound. At first it was decided simply to enlarge the church, and in 1452 Bernardo Rossellino was entrusted with the work by Nicholas V. He drew up a plan for the transformation of the area of the presbytery; but the consequent work was interrupted by the death of the pope in 1455, when the walls were still less than two metres high. It was Julius II (cf. p. 34) who decided to reconstruct the basilica completely. Donato Bramante was put in charge of the project; his conception was of a building in the form of a Greek cross framed by a square formed by four towers. There were to be four small cupolas and a large central one supported by a drum with windows; at

St. Peter's. The dome, detail of the drum.

the end of each arm of the cross there was to be a projecting semi-circular apse. On 18 April 1506 Julius II placed the first stone, at the foot of the pillar named after St. Veronica.

On the death of Bramante in 1514 only the central arches and four pillars had been completed. Leo X appointed Fra Giocondo da Verona and Giuliano da Sangallo to continue the work. On his death in 1515 Fra Giocondo was succeeded by Raphael, but the plan was changed: without destroying what Bramante had built they began to build a Latin cross. On the death of Raphael in 1520 the work was continued by his assistant Antonio da Sangallo and by Baldassarre Peruzzi. They returned to the Greek cross, but the work was interrupted again by the sack of Rome in 1527 and resumed under Paul III in 1534.

Antonio da Sangallo's wooden model of a building in the form of a Greek

St. Peter's. Interior of the dome.

cross was accepted. In order to allow services to be held in the nave, he separated it from the building area by a wall. The alterations that Sangallo made to Bramante's design impeded the progress of the work until 1540.

When Sangallo died, Paul III transferred the task to Michelangelo. In 1547 he allowed Michelangelo the freedom to alter the design as he saw fit, and in 1549 he appointed him architect for life of the fabric of the church.

Michelangelo decided to return to Bramante's design, into which he in-

troduced various changes made necessary, on the one hand by a different stylistic approach, and on the other by the need to give the whole structure a greater solidity. Despite continual difficulties, when Michelangelo died in 1564 the work was well in hand: the south transept was finished; the north transept and the drum for the cupola were almost finished. In 1564 Pius IV nominated Pirro Ligorio as chief architect of the fabric and Jacopo Vignola as second architect. But they were both opposed to Michelangelo's design, and were consequently dismissed in the following year. In 1567

St. Peter's. The aisles.

Vignola was recalled. He died in 1573 and was replaced by Giacomo della Porta who in 1588, under Sixtus V, began to construct the cupola. In 1590 the task was completed, and Gregory XIV ordered work to begin on the construction of the cleristory. In the papacy of Clement VIII, the bronze sphere was put in position. Clement entrusted the decoration of the cupola in mosaic to Cavalier d'Arpino, who was assisted by Cesare Nebbia and Giovanni Vecchi, among others.

What survived of the old basilica (the nave and aisles) was structurally precarious, and in 1605, under Paul V,

it began to be demolished. (The sepulchral monuments were preserved.) The question now arose of whether to continue with Michelangelo's design or to draw up a new plan for the church in the form of a Latin cross; it was in order to decide this that the pope now invited the most famous architects of the day to present their designs. It was Carlo Maderno's design that was adopted, in the form of a Latin cross. The construction of the nave and aisles began on 8 March 1607. In 1612 the facade was complete, and in 1615 the whole church was finished and ready for the admiration of the faithful.

Gian Lorenzo Bernini: Canopy over the papal altar above the tomb of St. Peter.

The problem remained of giving the required prominence to the tomb of St. Peter, which lay below the level of the new floor. (The new church was built on a higher level than Constantine's and, given the slope of the ground, on a higher level than the remains, still visible, of the pagan necropolis within which the apostle was buried.) Urban VIII Barberini (cf. p. 20) employed Bernini to build a canopy over the great altar. The work began on 19 June 1624. The bronze acquired from Livorno and from Venice proved to be insufficient, and so the artist suggested that the girders of the atrium and the ribbing of the cupola of the Pantheon be melted down. Hence the saying: "Quod non fecerunt Barbari fecerunt Barberini" (what the Barbarians left undone, was done by the Barberini). The quantity of bronze was such that, quite apart from the canopy, eighty cannons for the Castel Sant'Angelo were fashioned out of it. On 29 June 1633 the monument was consecrated. Four tendril-columns, on the model of those in Constantine's basilica, supported the canopy; they were decorated with bronze fringes and bronze tassels, and surmounted by four angels, by putti and by Barberini coats of arms. The casting was carried out by Gregorio de' Rossi under the direct supervision of Bernini; among Bernini's assistants was the young Francesco Borromini.

Antonio Averlino, known as Filarete: the central door of St. Peter's, detail with St. Paul and St. Peter handing over the keys to Eugene IV.

Antonio di Pietro Averlino (called "il Filarete") was summoned to Rome in 1433 to make the central bronze doors of St. Peter's — the first renaissance work in Rome. He was appointed to the task by Eugene IV Condulmer (1431-1447), who is represented next to St. Peter. The doors were placed in position on 14 August 1445; according to Giorgio Vasari the artist had worked on them for twelve years. Each door is decorated by three panels representing (on the left door) Christ enthroned, St. Paul, the condemnation and execution of St. Paul and his appearing to Plautilla; and on the right door the Virgin enthroned, St.

Peter giving the keys to Eugene IV, the condemnation and crucifixion of St. Peter. The four horizontal reliefs illustrate events of the papacy of Eugene IV. Above: the coronation of the Emperor Sigismund and the procession of pope and emperor to the Castel Sant'Angelo; the Council of Florence and the embarkation of the Greeks at Venice. Below (reproduced here): the arrival of John Palaeologue at Ferrara and his meeting with the pope; the Abbot Andreas receives from Eugene IV the decree for the unification of the eastern and western Churches and visits the tombs of St. Peter and St. Paul. In the ornamental border are mythological figures from Ovid, Livy, Valerius, Maximus and Virgil; indeed the influence of antiquity is evident in the style as well as the iconography of the doors. Several elements (for example the figures of the two apostles)

seem to be derived from palaeochristian art. The choice of themes represents the desire to celebrate the pope's attempts to achieve Christian unity. The two lower reliefs were added in 1620 by Paul V when the doors were incorporated in the new church; they had originally been made for Constantine's church.

The tomb of Pope Innocent VIII Cibo (1484-1492) is the work of Antonio del Pollaiuolo; he was commissioned to make it by Cardinal Innocenzo Cibo shortly after the pope's death. According to Vasari the work was begun in 1492 and had certainly been completed by 30 January 1498 when the remains of Innocent VIII were placed in it. The artist was probably assisted by his pupils, among whom was Piero del Pollaiuolo. Today the monument consists of the sarcophagus and above the sarcophagus the image of the pope giving his blessing, with the reliefs of Fortitude and Justice on the left, and Temperance and Prudence on the right. Above the monument is a lunette with reliefs of Hope, Charity and Faith.

In the old church the monument was arranged differently: from a drawing of the first few years of the seventeenth century (now in Berlin), we know that in fact the figure of the pope giving his blessing and the virtues on either side of him were placed under the sarcophagus, and that the whole monument was framed by a kind of marble triumphal arch; on the arch were pilaster-strips with the coat of arms of Innocent VIII at their base. In his left hand the pope holds the relic from the spear by which Christ was wounded on the cross, given to him in 1492 by Sultan Bajazet (1481-1512). It was in 1621 that the tomb was given its present form.

Antonio del Pollaiuolo: Tomb of Innocent VIII Cibo. St. Peter's.

Michelangelo: Pietà. St. Peter's.

The Pietà in St. Peter's is a youthful work of Michelangelo; he sculpted it between 1498 and 1500, for Cardinal Jean de Bilhères de Lagranlas, for the round Chapel of St. Petronilla in the old church of the Vatican. Michelangelo's protector the Roman banker Jacopo Galli stood as his guarantor; part of the contract runs: "And I Jacopo Galli promise the most reverent monsignor that the said Michelangelo will execute the said work in one year, and that it will be the most beautiful marble work in Rome, and that no master will make a better one." In the course of the centuries the Pietá was moved from one place to another. Finally, in 1749, Benedict XIV placed it where it is today, in the first chapel to the right of the entrance. In 1972 the Pietà was attacked and seriously damaged; it was restored successfully by the Restoration Laboratory of the Vatican Museums.

Medieval papal throne, kept in the throne by G. L. Bernini. St. Peter's.
◁
Gian Lorenzo Bernini: Throne and Apotheosis of the Holy Spirit. St. Peter's.

Among the works made by Bernini for St. Peter's is the magnificent reliquary in gilded bronze (the so-called throne of St. Peter, completed in the papacy of Alexander VII), a masterpiece of baroque art, which contains the wooden throne on which, according to tradition, the apostle sat. In the "edifice" conceived by Bernini (and set up in the church in 1666) the reliquary is supported by St. Augustine, St. Ambrose, St. Athanasius and St. John Chrysostom, symbols of the eastern and western Churches as subject to Rome. A burst of sunlight with clouds and angels surrounds the window, and on the window is an image of the Holy Spirit.

The throne contained in the reliquary does not really belong to the first century A.D. The ivory decoration can be dated to the ninth century; it consists of a series of friezes with plant volutes, classical in origin, sur-rounding small figures of men, animals and mixtures of man and animal. At the centre of the back is the bust of an emperor, probably Charles the Bald (823-877). The panels on the front of the seat are an addition; they represent fantastic animals and the labours of Hercules; their date is disputed, but they are probably of the ninth century and contemporary with Lothar. Originally the throne was kept in the monastery of St. Martin, which stood where now stands the pillar named after St. Veronica.

The tomb of Urban VIII Barberini (1623-1644) was made by Gian Lorenzo Bernini between 1628 and 1647; it is to be found in a recess in the apse of St. Peter's. The bronze image of the pope, seen as vicar of Christ and giving his blessing, rests on a high plinth; at the foot of the plinth is the sarcophagus, a work in marble and bronze; over the sarcophagus is the figure of Death with Charity and Justice on either side. Jurist, poet and patron of the arts, Urban VIII was for baroque Rome what Julius II and Leo X (cf. p. 34) had been for renaissance Rome; and as such, the artist he employed above all was Bernini.

The name that is connected with the creation of the Profane Museum of the Vatican Library is that of Clement XIII Rezzonico (1758-1769); he founded it in 1767 "Servandis Romanae Antiquitatis Monumentis" (for the preservation of the monuments of Roman antiquity) on the suggestion of the librarian Cardinal Alessandro Albani. Clement's tomb, also in St. Peter's, is the work of Antonio Canova, and was made between 1787 and 1792; the image of the pope praying rests on the sarcophagus, at the sides of which are representations of the Church and of the Spirit of Death.

The portrait of John XXIII Roncalli (1958-1963) appears in one of the panels of the Door of Death by Giacomo Manzù, which was placed in St. Peter's in 1964 at the first entrance on the left; the pope is represented praying and accompanied by the figures of Cain and Abel, St. Joseph, and Death in War.

△
Gian Lorenzo Bernini: Urban VIII Barberini, detail from his tomb. St. Peter's.
◁
Antonio Canova: Tomb of Clement XIII Rezzonico. St. Peter's.
▷
Giacomo Manzù: Door of Death, detail with John XXIII. St. Peter's.

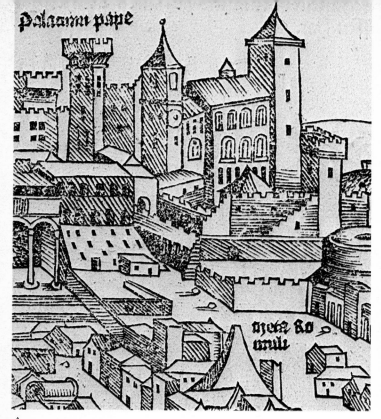

△
Hartmann Schedel: Medieval Apostolic Palace (detail from a map of Rome from 1493).
▷
Palace of Sixtus V. Sunday blessing from the pope's private apartments.
▷▷
Apostolic Palace. Courtyard of St. Damasus. To the left Bramante's Loggias and the medieval palace; in the centre the loggias of the Palace of Gregory XIII and to the right those of the Palace of Sixtus V.
▷▷
Marten van Heemskerck: Bramante's Loggias (detail from a drawing from 1533).

The Courtyard of St. Damasus opens onto the south towards St. Peter's Square. It is formed by three distinct buildings: to the west is the oldest nucleus of the Apostolic Palaces with the Loggias of Donato Bramante; to the north the wing of Gregory XIII and to the east the Palace of Sixtus V, from which the pope appears on religious festivals to give his blessing. The print by Hartmann Schedel of 1493 shows the Apostolic Palace before the work done by Bramante, with its towers and medieval fortification. The picture is of a collection of buildings of different periods built around the Courtyard of the Pappagallo. The south wing (which includes a building with a tower con-structed by Innocent III), with the Sala Ducale (cf. p. 27) and the Sala Regia, was constructed by Nicholas III, as was the east wing (which was later completed on the north side by Boniface VIII). Then there is the north wing, which was added by Nicholas V (cf. p. 28), with three towers at the corners (the north-west one was built by Alexander VI, cf. p. 30), and the Sistine Chapel, which had a defensive as well as a religious function. On the eastern facade, towards Rome, there were loggias even in the medieval building, and on the ground floor a portico. When Julius II (cf. p. 34) had the Belvedere Courtyard built he decided to decorate this eastern facade in renaissance style. Bramante began the work in about 1508. He closed the portico on the ground floor and replaced the two upper galleries with three rows of loggias, increasing thereby the height of the facade. A stairway on the south side with wide shallow steps (which in the nineteenth century Pius VII replaced with the ramp with landings and steps) joined Bramante's three Loggias. The work was finished by Raphael, who modified the project slightly by replacing the final loggia with a trabeated peristyle. The loggias of Gregory XIII, similar in every respect to Bramante's, are part of Gregory's Palace, and give onto the north side of the Courtyard of St. Damasus.

The Palace of Sixtus V, forming the east side of the Courtyard of St. Damasus, is the work of Domenico Fontana. It has a square plan with a rectangular courtyard in the middle, and to the north it joins the Palace of Gregory XIII. The facade giving onto the Courtyard of St. Damasus is an extension of the loggias; it had been begun by Martino Longhi, but was finished by Fontana.

On the second floor, in the Papal Suite (the "Appartamento Nobile Pontificio"), is the Clementine Hall (named after Clement VIII, who completed the construction begun by Sixtus V), possibly by Taddeo Landini. The room has a large "trompe l'œil" vault ceiling and frescoes by Giovanni and Cherubino Alberti and by Paul Bril. The Papal Suite was restored in 1964 by Dandolo Bellini. At its end, in the present Vatican Library, are landscape frescoes from the time of Paul V and paintings which were once in the Vatican Pinacoteca.

Apostolic Palace. Bronze Door. In the background the Portico of Constantine and the Scala Regia.
◁
The Papal Suite in the Palace of Sixtus V. Above: the Clementine Hall. Below: the pope's private library.

The main entrance to the Apostolic Palaces is through the Bronze Door, built in 1618 on a commission by Paul V, as is recorded in an inscription. The door is all that is left of the elaborate entrance built by Martino Ferrabosco and Jan van Xanten, later replaced by Bernini's Portico of Constantine (the long rectangular building on the right side of the basilica, cf. p. 6). At the end of this is the access to the Scala Regia,

with thirteen steps and a grand serliana crowned by two winged representations of Fame, holding the coat of arms of Alexander VII. On the right is the equestrian statue of Constantine, built by Bernini on a commission from Innocent X and, on the left, the entrance to the atrium of St. Peter's. The stairway connects the portico and the atrium to the Sala Regia; Antonio da Sangallo had built a stairway here earlier, but it was narrow, bare and badly lit. Alexander VII charged Bernini with the task of renovating it completely and this was put into effect between 1664 and 1666. The stairway is divided by a landing into two flights. The first is lined, so to speak, with an internal colonnade of Ionic style, supporting on its architrave a barrel-vault, which also serves the purpose of making more solid the

construction. The effect in perspective which is caused by the progressive lowering of the height of the vault, of the columns and also the narrowing of the width of the columns, allowed Bernini to camouflage the irregular, trapezoid, shape of the unit. The effect of perspective is emphasized by the light which falls almost entirely on the landing at the end of the first flight. The second flight is, on the other hand, only an adaptation of the stairway by Sangallo. Next to the Scala Regia, is the Scala dei Morti (the stairway of the dead), which derives its name from the fact that it is used for carrying the bodies of the popes into St. Peter's.

Medieval Apostolic Palace. Sala Ducale. In the foreground the "aula tertia", then the "aula secunda" and, in the background, the entrance to the Sala Regia.

◁
Gian Lorenzo Bernini: the first flight of the Scala Regia and the equestrian statue of Constantine. Apostolic Palace.

From the Sala Regia, "aula magna vel prima", one passes into the Sala Ducale, which comprises both the "aula secunda" and "tertia" (the latter, in the building of Innocent III, is the oldest part of the palaces); the present room is, in fact, the result of the union of two rooms, which in the medieval building were totally separate units. In the "aula tertia" the public consistory was held by the popes when they officially received those sovereign princes, or dukes, which in the Roman ceremonial are called the dukes of major power: hence the name of the room. In the sixteenth century, under Clement VII, the ceilings of the two rooms were lowered and covered with vaults and lunettes by Antonio da Sangallo. The work was continued by Paul III, and the decoration begun by Paul IV and finished by Gregory XIII. It is difficult to name with any certainty the artists who decorated the two rooms with grotesques, landscapes and stories. One scholar maintains that the landscapes in the frieze in the "aula tertia" are by Giovanni da Udine; the grotesques in the lunettes in the same room, on the south wall, are by Matteino da Siena, while the landscapes on the north wall were painted in this century, in the time of Benedict XV, and cover four little windows where once the ladies could watch the ceremony, on Holy Thursday, when the pope washed the feet of twelve poor priests dressed as apostles. In the seventeenth century, the two rooms were converted into a single one by Bernini on a commission from Alexander VII. The two rooms were not symmetrical and their shape was not regular, because the old medieval building had followed the shape of the neighbouring hillside. Bernini solved this problem by giving the opening between the two rooms an amusing curtain held up by two winged putti; the effect of this perspective correction is today partly lost, due to the geometrical designs on the marble floor, which replaced, under Benedict XV, the old tiles.

Medieval Apostolic Palace. Borgia Apartment. The Hall of the Saints with the stories of St. Barbara and St. Catherine of Alexandria. To the right in the foreground, Pius XII by Francesco Messina.
◁
Beato Angelico: St. Lawrence consecrated deacon by Sixtus II (portrait of Nicholas V). Niccoline Chapel. Medieval Apostolic Palace.

Fra Giovanni da Fiesole, called Beato Angelico, decorated the "cappella parva superior" in the tower of Innocent III on a commission by Nicholas V. This chapel is today known as the Niccoline Chapel. Angelico also frescoed the Studiolo of Nicholas V, between 1447 and 1449 and again between 1451 and 1454, about which we know very little. Between 1452 and 1455 he also frescoed the Chapel of St. Nicholas, next to the Sala Regia, which was later destroyed by Antonio da Sangallo in order to make room for the Scala del Maresciallo, then the main entrance to the Apostolic Palaces. Angelico had painted for Eugene IV (cf. p. 15), who had originally called him to Rome, another chapel in St.

Peter's probably between 1445 and 1449, but nothing is left of that. The Niccoline Chapel was painted between 1448 and 1451 and the two rows of frescoes depict stories from the lives of St. Stephen and St. Lawrence. The pope in these frescoes has the features of Nicholas V. In the corners the Doctors of the Church are portrayed, and on the ceiling are the four evangelists. As was usual in the fifteenth century, Angelico was most probably helped a great deal by apprentices and collaborators, among whom Benozzo Gozzoli, but the majority of the scenes were painted entirely by himself.

The Borgia Tower and Apartment date from the time of Alexander VI Borgia (cf. p. 30). This apartment, where the pope lived and died, occupies two rooms in the tower (the Halls of the Creed and of the Sibyls), the following three rooms (the Halls of the Mysteries, of the Saints and of the Liberal Arts), the Hall of the Popes in the northern wing, and a group of small rooms which can be reached through the Hall of the Liberal Arts in the west wing. The Hall of the Popes was used by the pope for official functions, while the Hall of the Liberal Arts served as his private study.

Bernardino Betti, called Pinturicchio, was entrusted with the decoration of these rooms; in 1492 he left Orvieto, where he was working in the Cathedral, and by 1494 had finished this work. The Hall of the Popes was not included in this decoration, and its ceiling was frescoed by Perin del Vaga and Giovanni da Udine, in the time of Leo X. In the Hall of the Mysteries of the Faith are depicted scenes from the incarnation and the resurrection of Christ. In the Hall of the Saints, there are scenes from the life of the Virgin and St. Sebastian, of Susanna, of St. Barbara, of St. Catherine of Alexandria and of St. Anthony Abbot and St. Paul Hermit. On the ceiling is the myth of Isis and Osiris and the bull Apis. In the Hall of the Liberal Arts are the allegories of the Trivium and the Quadrivium; in the Hall of the Creed, prophets and apostles; in the Hall of the Sibyls, prophets and sibyls. In this apartment today are exhibited the works of the Collection of Modern Religious Art, opened in 1973 by Paul VI, which includes works given to the pope by artists and collectors of our time.

Both Alexander VI's predecessor and his successor were members of the della Rovere family: Sixtus IV (1471-1484) and Julius II (1503-1513), both portrayed, the former as pope and the latter as cardinal, in the fresco of the Nomination of Bartolomeo Platina, in 1475, as prefect of the Vatican Library. Today this fresco is in the Pinacoteca, but it was intended as decoration for one of the halls which Sixtus IV had set aside to house the public library. This had been a project of Nicholas V, but was only realized by Sixtus IV. The rooms on the ground floor of the north wing of the Apostolic Palaces, below what was to become the Borgia Apartment, were used for this purpose. The first of these rooms housed the Latin Library and the second the Greek. These were followed by the Secret Library, with a collection of the most precious manuscripts, and the Pontifical Library, which held the papal archives and registers. Domenico and Davide del Ghirlandaio decorated the lunettes in the Latin Library with portrayals of the Fathers of the Church and classical philosophers, and Melozzo da Forlì painted the scene of the investiture of Platina on the wall between the two windows in this same room. In the Greek Libra-

ry, the decoration consists in a row of corinthian columns on the walls, and two portraits in the lunettes, perhaps teacher and disciple; but there is nothing left of the decoration of the next two rooms. A recent restoration has brought to the light the decoration on the ceiling of the Pontifical Library: an intricate, but stylized, floral decoration, in chiaroscuro, grey on a white background.

At the same time as he was creating the first library, Sixtus IV had the Palatine Chapel built, (1475-1483), later called the Sistine Chapel, by Giovannino de' Dolci, after a project by Baccio Pontelli.

The Sistine Chapel was built between 1475 and 1480, and by 1483 even the decoration on the walls was complete. Perugino was entrusted with its decoration; he began with the wall behind the altar, and also painted the now lost Annunciation. In 1481 he was joined by Sandro Botticelli, Domenico del Ghirlandaio and Cosimo Rosselli, and in the following year by Luca Signorelli, who completed the work. The frescoes are on three levels: on the first, painted tapestries, on the second, stories from the lives of Christ and Moses, and above this, the series of portraits of the popes.

The three popes (1484-1503) who succeeded Sixtus IV did not make any alteration to the chapel; but Julius II decided to have the ceiling frescoed by Michelangelo. The artist did not receive the order with any great pleasure, but nonetheless began work in May 1508. By September 1510 half the work was finished, and, on 14 August 1511, the pope insisted that it should be unveiled. By October of the following year, the work was finished and on the day of All Saints, Julius II inaugurated it with a solemn mass. The initial plan had consisted in twelve enormous figures of the apostles, but the artist had rejected this plan as unworthy. Given complete freedom of action, Michelangelo proceeded to create a monumental painted architectural structure, covering the real ceiling, but without any "trompe l'œil" intentions. In the nine large spaces thus created, he painted episodes from Genesis, from the creation to the drunkenness of Noah. In the corners of each scene are "Ignudi", and in the spaces between the side lunettes seven prophets alternate with five sibyls. In the four corners of the ceiling, he painted the stories of David and Goliath, of Judith and Holofernes, the punishment of Aman and the bronze serpent. In the lunettes above, are the ancestors of Christ, melancholy figures in expectation of the Messiah. Throughout this monumental task, Michelangelo refused any help and worked entirely alone.

Michelangelo: Frescoes on the ceiling of the Sistine Chapel.

Michelangelo: Detail from the Last Judgment. Sistine Chapel.

Twenty-one years later, in 1533, Clement VII called Michelangelo back to Rome to paint the Last Judgment on the wall behind the altar, and, in 1534, Paul III confirmed this commission. Once again the artist was very reluctant about the commission and waited two years before beginning the work. In order to make space for Michelangelo's fresco, Perugino's work had to be destroyed. On 31 October 1541, the scaffolding was removed and Paul III celebrated vespers beneath the monumental work, which filled Rome with "wonder and amazement". The unusual location of this subject matter had been suggested by Clement VII, who had wished to commemorate in this way the tragic events of the year 1527, the sack of Rome.

Medieval Apostolic Palace. Raphael's Stanze. Room of Heliodorus with the frescoes of the Mass at Bolsena and the portrait of Julius II, and the Meeting of Leo I (a portrait of Leo X) and Attila.

When Julius II became pope in 1503, he was very unwilling to occupy the Borgia Apartment and, in 1507, moved to the floor above. The Sala Vecchia degli Svizzeri was the entrance to the new apartment, the Room of the Chiaroscuri was the first antechamber, from which one passed into the pope's "cubiculum" and to the "stufetta", the bathroom. The actual apartment consisted in the Hall of Constantine and the three following rooms; the Hall of Constantine was used for official ceremonies, the Room of Heliodorus served as a secret ante-room, the Stanza della Segnatura was a private library, and the Room of the Fire in the Borgo was the usual dining room. Julius II ordered Raphael to decorate these rooms, destroying the previous decorations, among which, alas, a fresco by Piero della Francesca. Raphael frescoed the Stanza della Segnatura between 1508 and 1511 choosing as subject matter, probably on the pope's suggestion, the apotheosis of the supreme ideas: of revealed Truth (the Disputation of the Sacrament), of ra-

Giovanni da Udine: Raphael's work-shop, detail from the decoration of Bramante's second loggia. Medieval Apostolic Palace.

tional Truth (the School of Athens), of Beauty (Parnassus), and of the Good (portrayed by Virtue and the Law). In the Room of Heliodorus, paint-ed between 1511 and 1514, he re-presented Providence protecting the Church. In the Room of the Fire in the Borgo (1514-1517), for the most part painted by apprentices, there are a series of episodes illustrating popes who chose the name Leo, in homage to Leo X, who had become pope on the death of Julius II, in 1514. For the Hall of Constantine, Raphael pre-

pared a few drawings, but the actual decoration of the room is due to Giulio Romano and Giovanni Francesco Pen-ni, who worked on it between 1517 and 1524.

△▷
Medieval Apostolic Palace. Bramante's second loggia, known as Raphael's Loggia, looking north. Bramante's first loggia, known as Giovanni da Udine's Loggia, looking south.

Raphael worked on the Loggias both as painter and architect. He completed Bramante's project which, at the time of Leo X, stopped at the second loggia; Raphael added the third in order to complete the succession of the classical styles, each one on a different level. The project was begun in 1517 and completed in 1519. Raphael began on the second loggia, but never actually worked on the project himself, simply handing over drawings to his workshop, which included Giovanni da Udine, Giulio Romano, G. Francesco Penni, Perin del Vaga, and others of lesser renown. The decoration was for the most part derived from classical art, of which there were many examples in Rome, such as the "Domus Aurea". Giovanni da Udine in particular examined them with great care, attempting to reproduce them exactly even from the point of view of technique. In each vaulted ceiling classical and profane themes surround four scenes from the Old and New Testaments. In all there are fifty-two scenes, only four of which from the Gospels, which are known as Raphael's Bible. This loggia was

used by Leo X as his own private museum, where he placed numerous classical statues in the niches between the windows.

Giovanni da Udine also worked on the first loggia, which he finished after 1519. He painted on its ceilings "pergolas with vines heavy with bunches of grapes, with jasmine, with roses, and various kinds of animals and birds" (Vasari). Then, between 1560 and 1564, he decorated the third loggia, known as the Cosmographical Loggia, with grotesques, and allegorical stucco work.

Medieval Apostolic Palace. Third Loggia, known as the Cosmographical Loggia, looking north.

▷
Jan Matejko: John III Sobieski beneath the walls of Vienna (detail). Hall of Sobieski.

Between the Borgia Tower and the Apartment of St. Pius V lies the Hall of Sobieski, whose name derives from the enormous canvas by the Polish painter, Jan Matejko, depicting John III Sobieski, King of Poland, victorious against the Turks beneath the walls of Vienna in the battle of 1683. Sobieski had dedicated a good part of his life to the liberation of Europe from Turkish domination, and he formed a holy league with Pope Innocent XI and Emperor Leopold I to this end. His timely intervention in defense of Vienna was decisive for the victory of Christianity. This canvas, which occupies the entire north wall of the hall, is considered Matejko's great masterpiece. The painter, who dedicated his work almost exclusively to the illustration of historical subjects and the exaltation of his fatherland, refused to accept the payment of 80,000 florins for the canvas, so that on September 12, 1883, the date of the second centennial celebration of the glorious event represented therein, he might present it to Leo XIII. The presentation to the Pope is illustrated in a fresco in the Gallery of Candelabras.

Gallery of Maps.
▷
Ignazio Danti: Perspective map of Rome. Gallery of Maps.

The Gallery of Maps takes its name from the maps of the regions of Italy which were painted on its walls following the orders of Pope Gregory XIII in 1580. The dominican Ignazio Danti, a cosmographer, supplied the cartoons. It is in the west wing of the Belvedere Courtyard, above the corridor which contains the collections of the Vatican Library, on the same level as Raphael's Stanze. The task of building it was entrusted to the architect Ottaviano Mascherino probably around 1578. The gallery is 120 metres long and 6 wide; on the walls are rectangular windows and the ceiling is barrel-vaulted. At the centre of the wall on the courtyard side is an elegant "serliana" which opens onto a balcony. The attic above dates from the time of Urban VIII. Girolamo Muziano and Cesare Nebbia are responsible for the decoration of the ceiling, in which they were aided by many other artists. A letter written by Danti to the Flemish cosmographer Abraham Ortelius, is very useful in understanding the basic scheme of the frescoes: "...having divided Italy in half at the Apennines, I have placed on one side of the gallery that part which is bound by the Ligurian and Tyrrhenian seas, and on the other that which is bound by the Adriatic and the Alps, then subdividing the whole according to the states and the prefectures of the governments into fourty parts...". The most important cities are portrayed in perspective, as are the battles, in a felicitous figurative blend of history and geography. With reference to the other frescoes, he adds that they are "...eighty stories painted on the ceiling of the gallery, above each scene, representing some miracle known to have occurred in the region...". So that also on the ceiling we can see the mingling of history, in this case religious, and geography. In 1631, Urban VIII ordered the maps to be completed by the cosmographer Lucas Holstenius and enriched by new decorations.

ROMA

ER SACRAM B.PETRI SEDEM CAPVT ORBIS EFFECTA. S.LEO.

Library Courtyard. View of the rooms of the Secret Archive and the Tower of Winds. To the left, the Library of Sixtus V and, to the right, the Braccio Nuovo.

The Tower of Winds, the first astronomic observatory of the Vatican, dates from the time of Gregory XIII, and is connected to the reform of the calendar which was introduced by this pope in 1582. It was built above the Gallery of Maps (cf. p. 38) between 1578 and 1580, probably by Ottaviano Mascherino, the architect of the gallery. Overlooking the Library Courtyard, which used to be the middle level of the original Belvedere Courtyard, is a balcony made up of three terraces on different levels. The decoration in the rooms of the tower is the work of Niccolò Circignani, Mattheus Bril, and probably his brother Paul. Niccolò Circignani worked in the loggia which was to be the astronomic observatory, where he painted the personifications of the four winds. On the south wall he painted St. Peter's boat, on the west wall the shipwreck of St. Paul, two themes in a certain way connected ith the subject of winds. Mattheus Bril, perhaps with the help of his brother Paul, is the author of the sixty landscapes in the friezes in the other rooms.

△
Sacred Museum. View of Hall XI, called the Room of the Addresses. It contains a display of Roman and Early Christian glass, and cult objects from the Middle Ages to modern times in enamel, ivory and precious metals.

▷
The Galleria Lapidaria looking toward Bramante's first loggia. To the left (the east side, towards Rome) are the pagan inscriptions, and to the right the Christian ones.

The Galleria Lapidaria is the long corridor, with a flat ceiling, which connects the Chiaramonti Gallery in the Medieval Apostolic Palace, at the level of the first loggia, to the Palazzetto del Belvedere (cf. p. 44). Today it houses the Pio-Clementine Museum, in the east wing of the Belvedere Courtyard, this gallery was an indoor passage for the pope to his summer residence. This is also the part of the courtyard which has had fewer alterations. Raphael who began it and Antonio da Sangallo who finished it, both followed Bramante's original plan. Only in the seventeenth century, at the time of Urban VIII, was the original barrel-vaulted ceiling replaced with the present flat one. In the nineteenth century, under Pius VII, the Galleria Lapidaria was filled with the pagan and Christian inscriptions, these latter for the most part found in catacombs, which had previously been keps in the present Chiaramonti Gallery, the northern extension of the Galleria Lapidaria. This collection, which was the first nucleus of the Vatican Museums, had been begun in the previous century by

Clement XI and continued by Benedict XIV (cf. p. 57), who, after a suggestion by Giuseppe Bianchini, had placed it in the Chiaramonti Gallery. The new arrangement of this collection was supervized by Gaetano Marini, who placed the inscriptions in a thematical order. In this same form, we can today see about three thousand epigraphical documents from classical antiquity and late antiquity — perhaps the richest collection of its kind.

In the west wing, built in the 16th century by Pirro Ligorio on the opposite side of the Belvedere Courtyard, Benedict XIV established the Sacred Museum. It was situated beside the Vatican Library, in accordance with the ancient tradition which holds that libraries are not meant for the preservation of documents, manuscripts and prints alone, but must shelter and preserve every object which bespeaks antiquity.

Vatican Library. Salone Sistino.

The Sistine Library was built by Sixtus V to replace the one built by Sixtus IV, no longer large enough. Having discarded the initial plan to place it in Bramante's Corridor, the pope ordered the construction of a new building where the so-called Belvedere Theatre was. In this way the courtyard was cut in two, losing its unity once and for all. This decision was also taken in order to put a stop to those performances which Sixtus V thought unsuited to the dignity of the Apostolic Palace. The project was entrusted to Domenico Fontana in 1587, and in 1588 both the building and its decoration were complete. The speed with which the library was both built and decorated is typical of this pope: a saying of the time was, in fact, that the proverb "Dixit et facta sunt" was to be attributed to Sixtus V. In the eighteenth century the building underwent some changes on the ground floor, as is recorded by the following description by Fontana himself: "...it has enormous loggias on the ground floor, and behind them a very long cellar, above which are fourteen rooms on the second floor (today's Sezione del Catalogo), which will be given to eight men of letters who will always be able to study here...; on the third floor (today's Sala di Consultazione) there are eight rooms for the guardians of the library, and then the library itself (Salone Sistino), which is 318 palms long and 69 wide, with a row of columns in the middle and a vaulted ceiling; it has three rows of windows...; it is all beautifully painted with gold and with many stories...". The iconographical plan of the decoration of this room was arranged by the prefect of the library Federico Ranaldi, while the inscriptions are by the secret servant of the pope, Guglielmo Bianchi. The chosen themes were two: the glorification of the book through the centuries and the exaltation of the pontificate of Sixtus V. On one side of the library, the libraries of antiquity are

REX ROGAT ABBATEM MAThILDIM SupplICAT ATQ;

Miniature from the eleventh century. Henry IV, in the presence of Hugh Abbot of Cluny, begs Matilde of Canossa to intervene in his favour with Gregory VII in Canossa in 1077. Cod. Lat. 4922, Vatican Library.

portrayed, on the other the ecumenical councils whose task it had been to maintain learning on the road of truth; on the pilasters are the inventors of the letters of the alphabet. On the end wall and in the spaces above the windows are events from the pontificate of Sixtus V. One hundred painters, under the direction of Cesare Nebbia, who drew the cartoons, and Giovanni Guerra, who chose the subject matter, worked on this project. The scenes of Rome are by Paul Bril and Antonio Tempesta.

△
Palazzetto del Belvedere. The north facade. To the left, the tower of Bramante's Staircase and, to the right, the building of the Cabinet of Masks.

△
Anonymous copy of a drawing by Marten van Heemskerck (1535, detail). The Vatican Hill from north-west looking towards the Palazzetto del Belvedere.

▷
Pio-Clementine Museum. Above: the Gallery of Statues in the Palazzetto del Belvedere; in the foreground,

the plaque which marks the eastern boundary of Mantegna's Chapel, to the right, the former entrance to the Palazzetto, now walled up; in the background, beyond the arch, the Room of the Busts. Below: the Room of the Animals with the statue of Meleager.

The so-called Palazzetto del Belvedere was built for Innocent VIII (cf. p. 16) to the north of the Apostolic Palace, on the hill which was known in classical times as "mons sancti Aegidii". According to Vasari, Antonio del Pollaiuolo designed it, and Cristoforo da Pietrasanta, a Tuscan architect, built it between 1484 and 1487. The construction took place in two distinct phases. At first the building was conceived as a covered place where the pope, walking through the gardens, might stop for a rest. Later it was transformed into a villa. The original building was designed on a rectangular plan; the north facade had a tower on each side of it, a loggia on the ground floor, and a corresponding row of windows above it. The upper part of the building was crowned with "ghibelline" crenellations, rather unusual for a pontifical building, and in great contrast with the residential nature of the construction. The crenellations were on all sides of the palace, even on the south facade, now altered. As in many medieval buildings, the walls overlooking the slope of the hill were supported by massive stonework, with niches, as can be seen in the fresco, probably by Pinturicchio, in tre Gallery of Statues. When Innocent VIII decided to transform the building into a villa, a south wing was added to the south-eastern corner. The palace thus became L-shaped, and a few changes were made to the original building: two arcades in the eastern side of the loggia (to the

Courtyard of the Armour. The base of Antoninus' Column and the Atrium of the Four Gates.

left of the photograph), today the Gallery of Statues, were walled up to form the rooms of the papal residence; while, to the west, a small chapel with its own sacristy was built. Pinturicchio, who worked here around 1484, and Andrea Mantegna are responsible for the decoration of the Palazzetto del Belvedere. All that is left of the fifteenth century decoration are the frescoes on the ceiling, although later repainted, and the lunettes and fragments of flowers and fruit on the

wall opposite the windows in the Gallery of Statues. Between 1488 and 1490 Mantegna frescoed the small chapel which Innocent dedicated to St. John the Baptist. Vasari judged this work as "rather a work of miniature than painting", but there is nothing left of it.

Between the two fifteenth century wings of the palace there was a garden which Julius II decided to convert into his own private museum, open only to artists and men of letters. Donato Bramante worked on this project between 1510 and 1513. He built a wall along the east wing of tre palace, joining the north wing to the construction on the right of the Belvedere Courtyard. Parallel to the

east wall, he then built a loggia, also connected to both the buildings, creating a square courtyard, which he filled with orange trees. In the four corners he placed the famous statues of the Belvedere Apollo, the Venus Felice, the Tiber and the Laocoon group. Under Pius IV, the loggia of the courtyard was torn down and replaced by Pirro Ligorio with the two-storey building with the Room of the Animals on the ground floor and the Room of the Bronzes of the Gregorian Etruscan Museum on the first floor.

The Pio-Clementine Museum was begun by Clement XIV and completed by Pius VI. This museum incorporated, with slight alterations, the rooms of the Palazzetto of Innocent VIII and of

Pirro Ligorio: the Nicchione della Pigna.

the building of Pirro Ligorio, and led to the construction of new extensions. The first project was given, in 1771, to the architect Alessandro Dori who only made a very few changes; he transformed the loggia of the Palazzetto del Belvedere. into the Gallery of Statues, and demolished the dividing walls of the east wing, replacing them with the present arches which form the Room of the Busts, where Innocent VIII's small chambers had been. He also enlarged the west wing where the Cabinet of Masks now is. In 1772, Michelangelo Simonetti was

given the task of re-designing the contiguous Courtyard of the Oranges, giving it a portico. The architect followed the square plan of Bramante's courtyard, with its flattened corners, and made the octagonal portico, from which the present courtyard derives its name. The entrance was at the end of the Chiaramonti Gallery. On 12 May 1776, Pius VI decided that "this impressive construction should be completed by the addition of two more wings which would end in a round atrium, with access to the library". This task was intrusted to Simonetti, who was succeded at his death (1787) by his pupil Giuseppe Camporese, whose masterpiece is the Atrium of the Four Gates. The works began with the

demolition of the Mantegna chapel in order to prolong the Gallery of Statues. The room, at that time known as the Room of the Torso, was enlarged to the north and became the Room of the Animals. This room derives its name from the statues of animals, all classical but restored by Francesco Antonio Franzoni. This room was part of the building of Pirro Ligorio, and now houses the statue of Meleager. Lastly, the west wing of the Gallery of Statues was transformed into the Cabinet of Masks, a typical eighteenth century museum.

△▷
Gregorian Etruscan Museum. Above: Golden Etruscan diadem (fourth century B.C.). Below: Crater from Paestum (350-325 B.C.) depicting Zeus who, with the complicity of Hermes, is courting Alcmene.
◁
Gregorian Egyptian Museum. Room III. Roman statues of Egyptian inspiration. Egyptian style wall decoration of the last century.

The Gregorian Etruscan Museum, 1837, and the Gregorian Egyptian Museum, 1839, both founded by Gregory XVI, are housed in the buildings behind the Nicchione by Pirro Ligorio, and in the side wings, built under Julius II, Julius III and Pius IV by Donato Bramante, Girolamo da Carpi and Pirro Ligorio, which partially overlook the Octagonal Courtyard.

The Etruscan Museum, which also spreads to the upper floor of the Palazzetto del Belvedere (cf. p. 44), has a collection of objects for the most part found in the necropoles of southern Etruria, in private digs licensed by the Pontifical Government.

The Egyptian Museum is important not only for the objects it exhibits, but also for the attempt, at the time unheard of, to recreate entire rooms. The new arrangement of the museum, which strictly follows modern theories, has very rightly respected the romantic, naive, but for the time very daring, nineteenth century pseudo-Egyptian decoration by Giuseppe de Fabris.

*Donato Bramante: Spiral Staircase.
Palazzetto del Belvedere.*
▷
*Fountain of the Galley at the foot
of Bramante's Spiral Staircase.*

Next to the east facade of the Palazzetto del Belvedere (cf. p. 44) there still stands a tower, very rustic in appearance, with unplastered stonework, without any decoration, with four windows on different levels on the east and west sides, and only one on the north. This tower encloses the Spiral Staircase built by Bramante. It had been built as a separate entrance to the building and survived the eighteenth century modernizations intact, unlike the rest of the Palazzetto del Belvedere. This staircase winds up from the right to the left, and is paved in brickwork in a herringbone pattern. The barrel-vaulted ceiling is supported by the bare wall with small niches on the outside and by a continuous row of columns on the inside of the staircase. These columns are of different styles: Doric, at the beginning of the staircase, Ionic, at the middle, and Corinthian, at the top. The height of the columns remains the same throughout, while the distance between one column and the next decreases from the bottom towards

the top, to give the impression that the staircase is in fact higher than it is. Bramante often uses this method of false perspective. The only allusion to Julius II, the reigning pope, are the branches of oak, the symbol of the della Rovere family, on the last Doric capital. On the last floor, the staircase ends abruptly, without any conclusive elements, and this can perhaps be explained by the fact that Bramante did not personally complete the work. The staircase, begun around 1512, was continued by Baldassarre Peruzzi under Paul III and completed by Pirro Ligorio around 1564.

To the left of the entrance of the Spiral Staircase, there is a very pretty fountain with a lead galley in the centre and the water spurts out of its cannons. It is called the Fountain of the Galley and was built by Carlo Maderno in the reign of Paul V; Clement IX had the galley from which it derives its name placed in its centre.

△
Jan van Xanten, known as Vasanzio: Fontana dell'Aquilone. Vatican Gardens.

▷
Vatican Gardens. The Gardener's House, built around a tower which was probably part of the walls of Innocent III.

▷▷
Jan van Xanten, known as Vasanzio: Fountain of the Sacrament. Vatican Gardens (behind the Mint, where one of the gates of the old Leonine walls had been).

To the west of the Belvedere Courtyard (cf. p. 56) are the Vatican Gardens, which were begun in the sixteenth century. Pius IV ordered the construction of the Casina Pia and Paul V took great interest in the gardens, commissioning many fountains, especially from Martino Ferrabosco, among which the Fountain of the Mirrors. He also had the building above this fountain built (the Mint), which spans the Stradone ai Giardini, providing a direct communication between the palace and the gardens.

Vatican Gardens. Casina of Pius IV.
▷
Vatican Gardens. Casina of Pius IV. Above left: view of the loggia. Above right: facade of the villa. Center: upper facade of the loggia (above), and the Papal Academy of Science (below). Below left: back facade of the Papal Academy of Science. Below right: interior of the villa.

The Casina of Pius IV (Casina Pia) was built as a resting place for the popes, as a replacement for the one built by Innocent VIII (cf. p. 44) which had become a museum and a hostel for artists. It was begun under Paul IV, perhaps in 1558, by Pirro Ligorio and finished in 1561, under Pius IV. The Casina is in the Vatican Gardens and is surrounded by a high wall. It. consists in two constructions, the villa itself and a loggia, separated by an elliptical courtyard, enclosed by a wall topped with pots, with two entrances, at the north and at the south sides. The loggia and the villa are on the same level, while the courtyard is slightly lower. The external facade of the loggia is crowned by a tympanum, while the lower part of the construction appears to come out of a pool of water which surrounds the building on three sides. A second fountain is in the centre of the courtyard, in front of the facade of the villa, richly decorated with stuccoes

classical in style and subject matter, which also decorate the inside facade of the loggia.

The villa is on two storeys, and a cellar, and actually the division of the facade into three levels of decoration is purely ornamental. This was done in order to make the villa appear "grander and with more apartments and rooms than there actually were" (G. P. Chattard). In contrast to the relatively simple plan of the building, the decoration, like that of the loggia, is very elaborate. Lorenzo Costa, Federico Barocci, Santi di Tito and Federico Zuccari, were all called on to fresco the villa, while the stuccoes of the facade are the work of Rocco da Montefiascone. The works, begun in 1560, ended in 1563. During this century, a building was added onto the Casina Pia, to house the Papal Academy of Science, founded by Pius XI in 1936.

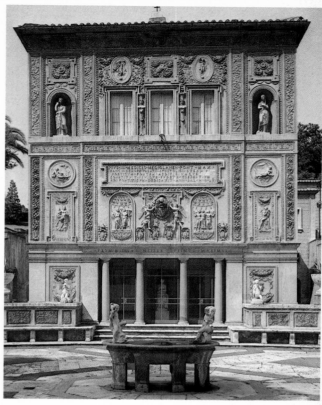

To the right: the Sistine Chapel, the building of Pius V and the Borgia Tower; in the background, the Belvedere Courtyard planned by Bramante and built by him and Ligorio (later it was modified and divided into two parts by the Library of Sixtus V and by the Braccio Nuovo); to the left is the Tower of Winds and the Nicchione della Pigna by Ligorio behind it. Above left: the Four Gates and the Pinacoteca, the Casina of Pius IV and, further to the right, the Stradone ai Giardini and the Fountain of the Mirrors at the foot of the building of Paul V. In the foreground the Mint and the Square of the Furnace.

The Belvedere Courtyard was designed by Bramante in order to provide an easy access from the Apostolic Palace to the Palazzetto del Belvedere (cf. p. 44) of Innocent VIII, which was on a higher level on the "mons sancti Aegidii". The space between the two, a large area surrounded by walls cultivated with vineyards and vegetable gardens, was difficult and uncomfortable to cross. Bramante planned to connect the two buildings with two

long, parallel corridors, with many levels, topped by a terrace, almost like a raised road, which would have connected the second loggia (cf. p. 36) of the Apostolic Palace to the first floor of the Belvedere. This terrace was to have been intended for horses as well. The highest covered gallery, which still stands today (cf. p. 41), connected the first loggia of the palace (cf. p. 36) to the Courtyard of the Oranges, today the Octagonal Courtyard. The lower galleries were shorter, because the Belvedere Courtyard was on three different levels, which compensated for the different height of the two buildings. The connection between these different levels was through monumental staircases, of which few traces remain today. The construction of the library of Sixtus V (cf. p. 42) and, much later, of the Braccio Nuovo, at the end of the middle level, involved the demolition of these staircases and the division of the original courtyard into the three present ones, the Belvedere Courtyard, the Library Courtyard and the Courtyard of the Pigna. On the lower level jousts, games and plays took place, which the public watched from the windows of the palace or from the steps of the stair-

case which led to the middle level. This was kept as a garden, like the upper one, which ended with a facade with an exedra at the centre and corinthian columns alternating with niches. The exedra did not cover the upper part of the Palazzetto del Belvedere which could be reached by a staircase of sixteen steps, eight concave and eight convex. The side galleries opened out like a portico on the upper and lower levels. The lower one was, however, closed and modified by Antonio da Sangallo under Paul III for reasons of stability. Bramante, who began the work in 1504, only partially completed the project, having laid only the foundations for the entire west wing. The work was continued by Raphael, Antonio da Sangallo, and later by Pirro Ligorio who, under Pius IV, completed the project with substantial modifications, such as the construction of the Nicchione (cf. p. 47), which replaced the exedra by Bramante.

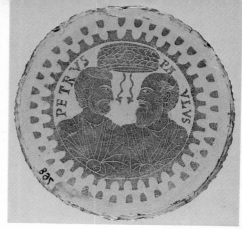

Giuseppe Maria Crespi: Benedict XIV Lambertini. Vatican Pinacoteca.

Giuseppe Maria Crespi painted this portrait when Prospero Lambertini was still a cardinal and the archbishop of Bologna. When he became pope with the name of Benedict XIV, in 1740, Lambertini wrote to Crespi instructing him to clothe him in white and to send the portrait to the Vatican. Crespi followed the instructions, even adding an extremely ornate tiara, but the work was done in a great hurry and, underneath the white papal robes, the cardinal's red is still visible. Benedict XIV was a very cultured man who patronized the arts. He founded the present Pontifical Academy of Archeology and, realizing a project of Clement XI, he set up, in 1756, the Sacred Museum of the Vatican Library, "ad augendum Urbis splendorem et asserendam Religionis veritatem" (to increase the splendor of the City and assert the truth of the Religion). He also founded the Galleria Lapidaria (cf. p. 41), originally located in the northern part of Bramante's Corridor, now the Chiaramonti Museum.

Sacred Museum. Early Christian glass cup with the images of St. Peter and St. Paul tooled in gold leaf.

Sacred Museum. The Annunciation on a silk ground, from the christian countrys in the East. 7th-8th centuries.

Giotto and his school: Stefaneschi triptych (back), St. Peter enthroned with saints and angels. Vatican Pinacoteca.

The Stefaneschi triptych in the Vatican Pinacoteca was painted by Giotto for St. Peter's basilica where it remained until 1932, even though not in its original place, the sacristy of the basilica. Giotto painted it for Cardinal Jacopo Gaetani degli Stefaneschi, perhaps for the main altar of the basilica. The date is uncertain, but probably around 1315. It is certain that the Florentine master was helped by numerous assistants, among whom perhaps the Maestro delle Vele, but the figures of the central panel are probably by Giotto, as is the Madonna with angels and saints in the predella. The triptych is made up of three panels of poplar wood. On the central one is Christ giving his blessing, seated on a throne surrounded by angels and with Cardinal Stefaneschi kneeling in worship before him, with his red cardinal's hat at his feet. The left panel is the representation of the crucifixion of St. Peter, and the right one the decapitation of St. Paul. On the back is St. Peter enthroned, with two angels at his side, and, at his feet, St. George who is presenting the cardinal in the act of offering the triptych, and Pope St. Silvester, who is placing into his care the hermit Pietro da Murrone, elected pope with the name Celestine V, here with a halo and therefore already dead, who is in the act of offering a codex, perhaps the codex of St. George, now in the Vatican Library. On the back of the side panels are, on the left one, St. James and St. Paul and, on the right one, St. Andrew and St. John the Evangelist. On the front of the predella is the Madonna and Child with two angels and the apostles James and Peter in the centre, and the other ten at the sides. On the back, all that is left are a St. Stephen, a St. John the Evangelist and a St. Lawrence. Since the side with St. Peter enthroned appeared more damaged by smoke in a recent restoration than the side with Christ, it is probable that this was the side which originally faced the altar.

Raphael and Pieter van Aelst: Tapestry representing the miraculous haul of fishes, detail. Vatican Pinacoteca.

The tapestries of the "Old School" kept in the Vatican Pinacoteca were commissioned in 1515 from Raphael by Leo X, who wanted to decorate the walls of the Sistine Chapel with them on solemn occasions. These tapestries were hung in the presbytery, under the frescoes from the lives of Christ and Moses, and were first shown to the public on 26 December 1519. Raphael designed the cartoons, now kept at the Victoria and Albert Museum in London, between 1515 and 1516. Pieter van Aelst made the tapestries in Brussels. Among those who helped Raphael, the hand of Perin del Vaga is recognizable in the grotesques on the side bands. The cycle is composed of ten scenes from the Acts of the Apostles. The tapestries are called of the "Old School" to distinguish them from the "New School", in which episodes from the Gospels are depicted. These were also made by Pieter van Aelst, but only after Raphael's death, from cartoons drawn up by apprentices. Today these tapestries are in the Gallery of Tapestries.

Missionary - Ethnological Museum. Statue of Bhima, the benevolent demon (southern India).
◁
Gregorian Profane Museum. Room of the Asaroton mosaic.
◁
Pio-Christian Museum.

One of the most recent constructions in the Vatican, inaugurated in 1970, now houses the collections formerly in the Lateran. These include the Gregorian Profane Museum, the Pio-Christian Museum and the Missionary-Ethnological Museum. The Gregorian Profane Museum was set up by Gregory XVI in 1844 and includes mainly ancient sculptures, copies and remodellings of classical Greek originals and also Roman sculptures from the late republican and imperial eras. The Pio-Christian Museum was founded by Pius IX in 1854. In it are collected works of early Christian art, particularly sarcophagi and inscriptions. Lastly, the Missionary-Ethnological Museum was set up by Pius XI in 1927 and houses documents of religions other than the Christian, of non-European art and cultures. According to the wishes of

John XXIII, these museums were transferred to a building to the north of the Pinacoteca. Begun in 1963-1964 by Vatican architects, this building was then transformed between 1964 and 1971 by the architectural firm of the Passarelli brothers. The south wall, with its squat and protruding arches, is reminiscent of the earlier "wall of the spinster". The interior consists of one large room. The Gregorian Profane Museum is on the ground floor, while the Pio-Christian is raised on a sort of balcony on the same floor. Metal trellisses are the dividing walls, and metal tubes form the pedestals of the sculptures, enhancing even more their shape and form in the contrast with these amorphous objects. The arrangement of the material is didactic as it is in the Missionary-Ethnological Museum, on the floor beneath.

Historical Museum.
▷
Pier Luigi Nervi: Hall of Papal Audiences.
▷▷
St. Peter's Square. Christmas blessing "Urbi et Orbi".

The Historical Museum, opened to the public in 1973, was set up below the so-called Square Garden next to the Pinacoteca. The carriages and other means of transport used by the popes and by their following, from the nineteenth century till the present day, are exhibited in this museum, together with various uniforms and relics of the papal armed forces, disbanded in 1970.

The Hall of Papal Audiences is another very recent construction, designed by Pier Luigi Nervi in 1964 and inaugurated in 1971. It can hold 12,000 people and is shell-shaped. The immense vaulted ceiling is structurally bound to the concave gallery, forming a solid body which almost "floats" on the unsteady ground.

MONUMENTI MUSEI E
GALLERIE PONTIFICIE